With love to our little angel, Zach
~ Mimi

# THE WISE ANIMAL HANDBOOK

Kate B. Jerome

ARCADIA KIDS

Attempt new **skills** from **time** to **time.**

Just **try** to think them **through.**

And if you **find** you're left
**behind...**

...then change your point of view.

Try
not
to
think
of just
yourself.

Invent new ways to share.

Stay close to friends whom you can trust.

But
always
be
aware.

# Avoid the tattle in the tale.

Insist that **truth** is **best**.

# Embrace with pride the strengths you have.

**Demand to be impressed.**

# Enjoy the peace that nature brings.

Ignore what's just for show.

Join **forces** when the road gets **rough.**

Admit when you don't know.

Remember
**family**
is the
**best.**

Despite the ups and downs.

# Don't **hide** from things that you must **face.**

Make
joyful
laughing
sounds.

Eat **healthy** food to **grow** up **strong.**

Be patient with your friends.

# Try not to take a stubborn stand.

Be
quick
to make
amends.

Excuse yourself when **manners** slip.

Be **helpful** every **day.**

Keep **trying** even when it's **hard.**

But
don't
forget to
play!

# And sing

...and **dance** each **day!**

Written by Kate B. Jerome
Design and Production: Lumina Datamatics, Inc.
Coloring Illustrations: Tom Pounders
Research: Eric Nyquist

Cover Images: See back cover

Interior Images: 002 Anetapics/Shutterstock.com; 003 George Green/Shutterstock.com; 004 Sergey Uryadnikov/Shutterstock.com; 005 Gnomeandi/Shutterstock.com; 006 Bruce MacQueen/Shutterstock.com; 007 Henk Bentlage/Shutterstock.com; 008 M.M./Shutterstock.com; 009 Mikael Damkier/Shutterstock.com; 010 Brendan van Son/Shutterstock.com; 011 Michael Pettigrew/Shutterstock.com; 012 StevenRussellSmithPhotos/Shutterstock.com; 013 Pakhnyushchy/Shutterstock.com; 014 Patjo/Shutterstock.com; 015 Quinn Martin/Shutterstock.com; 016 Lincoln Rogers/Shutterstock.com; 017 Dirk Ercken/Shutterstock.com; 018 Karel Gallas/Shutterstock.com; 019 Orangecrush/Shutterstock.com; 020 Guenter-foto/Shutterstock.com; 021 Janecat/Shutterstock.com; 022 Shironina/Shutterstock.com; 023 Annette Shaff/Shutterstock.com; 024 Vitaly Titov/Shutterstock.com; 025 Rohappy/Shutterstock.com; 026 MattiaATH/Shutterstock.com; 027 Otsphoto/Shutterstock.com; 028 FikMik/Shutterstock.com; 029 Four Oaks/Shutterstock.com; 030 Ekaterina Kolomeets/Shutterstock.com; 031 Hugh Lansdown/Shutterstock.com.

Published by Arcadia Kids, a division of Arcadia Publishing and
The History Press, Charleston, SC

For all general information contact Arcadia Publishing at:
Telephone: 843-853-2070
Email: sales@arcadiapublishing.com

For Customer Service and Orders:
Toll Free: 1-888-313-2665
Visit us on the Internet at www.arcadiapublishing.com

Library of Congress Cataloging-in-Publication data is on file with the publisher.

Printed in China

# Iowa State **Bird**

## Eastern Goldfinch

**Read Together**

The eastern goldfinch was named the state bird in 1933. This brightly-colored bird is commonly seen throughout the state.

# An Iowa **Butterfly**

## The Monarch

**Read Together**

As the monarch butterfly becomes more rare, lots of people throughout Iowa are working to find ways to protect this beautiful insect.

# An Iowa **Mammal**

## The White-Tailed Deer

**Read Together**

White-tailed deer are found throughout Iowa. Did you know that male deer, called bucks, shed their antlers and grow new ones every year?

# An Iowa **Amphibian**

## The North American Bullfrog

**Read Together**

The bullfrog is the largest frog found in Iowa. When it stretches out its legs, it can be over a foot long!